Women Writers

A BOOK OF POSTCARDS
Photographs by Jill Krementz

Pomegranate

SAN FRANCISCO

Pomegranate
Box 6099
Rohnert Park, CA 94927

Pomegranate Europe Ltd.
Fullbridge House, Fullbridge
Maldon, Essex CM9 7LE
England

ISBN 0-87654-899-0
Pomegranate Catalog No. A823

Pomegranate publishes books of
postcards on a wide range of subjects.
Please write to the publisher for more information.

Designed by Elizabeth Key
Printed in Korea
06 05 04 03 02 01 00 99 98 97   11 10 9 8 7 6 5 4 3 2

As a young woman, Jill Krementz quickly established herself as one of America's most talented photojournalists. Even while cutting her teeth as a reporter, columnist, and photographer for various New York–based publications—including the *New York Herald Tribune*, which hired her in 1964 as its first female (and youngest) staff photographer—Krementz displayed a passionate and unique visual style.

Now the author of numerous books of photo essays—most notably two award-winning series for children and young adults—Krementz has long had a special affinity for writers. Although this developed quite naturally from her lifelong love of reading, what began as a bibliophile's attempt "to carve out a little niche for myself" has grown into a massive, and unrivaled, photographic archive of contemporary literary figures. Dating back to 1961 and comprising sessions with more than 1,500 writers, her collection is not just a visual feast for modern book lovers; it will also undoubtedly serve as an invaluable resource for future scholars, not unlike Carl Van Vechten's photographic collection of Harlem Renaissance writers of the 1920s and 1930s.

Uncompromising and thorough in her preparation, Jill Krementz brings to each session a familiarity with her subject's work. This sensitivity allows her, according to one reviewer, "to convey her subject's literary style as well as that person's physical image." Each of the thirty images of literary women contained herein was selected by the photographer as the most representative from her session with that writer. ■

Women Writers

PHOTOGRAPHS BY JILL KREMENTZ

MAYA ANGELOU, Winston-Salem, N.C., April 4, 1994
Maya Angelou (b. 1928), poet, playwright, and professor, has said, "I speak to the black experience, but I am always talking about the human condition." This was made clear to millions when she read one of her poems at Bill Clinton's inauguration. Her autobiographical prose and poetry have been collected in several volumes, including *I Know Why the Caged Bird Sings* (1970).

POMEGRANATE BOX 6099 ROHNERT PARK CA 94927

Women Writers

PHOTOGRAPHS BY JILL KREMENTZ

ANAÏS NIN, New York, N.Y., June 3, 1971
Born in Paris and raised in America by parents of Spanish, Danish, and
French lineage, Anaïs Nin (1903–1977) returned to Paris in 1923 and
began a lifelong "fantasy voyage" in such "antinovels" as *Winter of Artifice*
(1936) and in short erotica. Though her seven-volume *Diary* (published
1966–1978) brought Nin fame, all her work is highly personal and
universally feminine.

POMEGRANATE   BOX 6099   ROHNERT PARK   CA   94927

Women Writers

PHOTOGRAPHS BY JILL KREMENTZ

JANET FLANNER, New York, N.Y., January 21, 1975
Under the byline "Genêt," Janet Flanner (1892–1978) sent dispatches
from Paris to the *New Yorker* for half a century. She was the center of an
expatriate circle that included Kay Boyle, Gertrude Stein, and Djuna
Barnes, portraits of whom appear in such memoir/anthologies as *Paris
Was Yesterday* (1972).

POMEGRANATE   BOX 6099   ROHNERT PARK, CA 94927

Women Writers

PHOTOGRAPHS BY JILL KREMENTZ

JOAN DIDION, Trancas, Calif., March 31, 1972
Joan Didion (b. 1934) has turned her deft, unsentimental prose to fiction and journalism, seeking what she calls "controlled perfection." She is best known for her brilliant and incisive reportage and essays in *Slouching Toward Bethlehem* (1968), *The White Album* (1979), and *Salvador* (1983).

POMEGRANATE BOX 6099 ROHNERT PARK CA 94927

Women Writers

PHOTOGRAPHS BY JILL KREMENTZ

GWENDOLYN BROOKS, New York, N.Y., November 13, 1993
With her gently insightful poetry, Gwendolyn Brooks (b. 1917) has earned
some fifty honorary degrees; a Pulitzer Prize, for *Annie Allen* (1949); the
Illinois Laureateship (succeeding Carl Sandburg); and the Consultantship
in Poetry at the Library of Congress. She still lives near where she grew up—
the South Side of Chicago, the setting for much of her verse.

POMEGRANATE BOX 6099 ROHNERT PARK CA 94927

Women Writers

PHOTOGRAPHS BY JILL KREMENTZ

JANE SMILEY, New York, N.Y., November 13, 1991
Jane Smiley (b. 1949) has probed family life, labor, and trauma in eight works of fiction that linger powerfully in the reader's mind. A versatile writer and teacher, she won a Pulitzer Prize for *A Thousand Acres* (1991), the story of a King Lear–like farmer and his abused daughters, and followed that with *Moo* (1995), a brilliant satire of modern academia.

POMEGRANATE BOX 6099 ROHNERT PARK CA 94927

Women Writers

PHOTOGRAPHS BY JILL KREMENTZ

KATHERINE ANNE PORTER, College Park, Md., October 13, 1972
Born into poverty in Texas, Katherine Anne Porter (1890–1980) moved to
Chicago to study acting after the breakup of a teenage marriage. Self-
educated and fiercely independent, Porter wandered the world, living in
places as far-flung as Berlin, Bermuda, and Hollywood. She wrote brilliant
short stories and a classic novel, *Ship of Fools* (1962).

POMEGRANATE BOX 6099 ROHNERT PARK CA 94927

Women Writers

PHOTOGRAPHS BY JILL KREMENTZ

TONI MORRISON, New York, N.Y., February 13, 1974
Toni Morrison (b. 1931) creates richly textured prose that mines her experience as an African American woman in a predominantly white society. For her entire body of work—from her first novel, *The Bluest Eye* (1970), through *Jazz* (1992)—she was awarded the 1993 Nobel Prize in literature.

POMEGRANATE BOX 6099 ROHNERT PARK, CA 94927

Women Writers

PHOTOGRAPHS BY JILL KREMENTZ

MARGARET ATWOOD, Toronto, Ont., Canada, June 25, 1994
Margaret Atwood (b. 1939) has spent most of her life in Canada, though she is internationally acclaimed for both poetry and fiction. Among her best-known works are the controversial and subversively visionary novels *Life Before Man, The Handmaid's Tale,* and *The Robber Bride.*

POMEGRANATE BOX 6099 ROHNERT PARK CA 94927

Women Writers

PHOTOGRAPHS BY JILL KREMENTZ

MAY SARTON, York, Maine, April 8, 1975

May Sarton (1912–1995) pursued her muse prolifically and with fierce independence. Her fiction, verse, and journals were part of a singular quest for solitude, which she found on the coast of Maine. Though autobiographical, works like *Mrs. Stevens Hears the Mermaids Singing* (1965), *The House by the Sea* (1977), and *Halfway to Silence* (1980) have struck a chord in her loyal following.

POMEGRANATE BOX 6099 ROHNERT PARK CA 94927

Women Writers

PHOTOGRAPHS BY JILL KREMENTZ

KAYE GIBBONS, Raleigh, N.C., April 5, 1994

Kaye Gibbons (b. 1960) joined the front rank of southern writers with her first novel, *Ellen Foster,* winning lavish praise from such venerable peers as Eudora Welty and Walker Percy. She has sustained her "good ear" and "good heart" in three novels since, most recently in *Sights Unseen.*

POMEGRANATE   BOX 6099   ROHNERT PARK, CA 94927

Women Writers

PHOTOGRAPHS BY JILL KREMENTZ

RITA DOVE, Charlottesville, Va., March 4, 1995
Rita Dove (b. 1952) has won numerous awards for her verse, including
a Pulitzer Prize for *Thomas and Beulah* (1987), a story-poem about her
grandparents. In 1993 she was appointed U.S. Poet Laureate, becoming
the youngest poet and the first African American to receive this honor.

POMEGRANATE BOX 6099 ROHNERT PARK CA 94927

Women Writers

PHOTOGRAPHS BY JILL KREMENTZ

ALICE MUNRO, Clinton, Ont., Canada, June 8, 1984
Alice Munro (b. 1931) has used her personal experience of small-town
Canada to create a fictional universe that has been described as "a kind
of magic." Primarily a writer of loosely linked short stories, Munro
began attracting worldwide notice in 1984 with *The Beggar Maid*.

POMEGRANATE   BOX 6099   ROHNERT PARK CA 94927

Women Writers

PHOTOGRAPHS BY JILL KREMENTZ

ROSELLEN BROWN, New York, N.Y., May 21, 1995
Rosellen Brown (b. 1939) writes and teaches prose and poetry. Ordinary
people are transformed by extraordinary circumstances in her writing,
most notably in the novels *Civil Wars* (1984) and *Before and After* (1992).

POMEGRANATE BOX 6099 ROHNERT PARK CA 94927

Women Writers

PHOTOGRAPHS BY JILL KREMENTZ

CATHLEEN SCHINE, New York, N.Y., April 22, 1995
Cathleen Schine (b. 1953) is a rare combination of intellectual and satirist, creating complex novels of ideas that are highly readable and outlandishly funny. Her *Rameau's Niece* (1993) was described as "our cousinly reply to A. S. Byatt, and the sex is better."

POMEGRANATE BOX 6099 ROHNERT PARK CA 94927

Women Writers

PHOTOGRAPHS BY JILL KREMENTZ

TERRY McMILLAN, New York, N.Y., April 29, 1995
Terry McMillan (b. 1951) is an uninhibited and wildly funny writer whose tales of manners among modern African American women (*Disappearing Acts, Waiting to Exhale*) have quickly achieved mass success. She is also in demand for her enthralling readings of her work.

POMEGRANATE   BOX 6099   ROHNERT PARK CA 94927

Women Writers

PHOTOGRAPHS BY JILL KREMENTZ

M. F. K. FISHER, Sonoma, Calif., May 25, 1983

M. F. K. Fisher (1908–1992) grew up in California but was transformed into a "serious gourmand" by France, where she moved in 1929. She used both settings—and the metaphor of food—to reflect on and savor the details of life. Her gastronomic writings are collected in *The Art of Eating* (1954) and *A Cordiall Water* (1961), and her memoirs are gathered in several much-cherished volumes.

POMEGRANATE   BOX 6099   ROHNERT PARK CA 94927

Women Writers

PHOTOGRAPHS BY JILL KREMENTZ

ANNE SEXTON, New York, N.Y., November 11, 1968
Anne Sexton (1928–1974) was an exceptionally gifted poet who struggled with "madness" most of her adult life, a literary battle that began with *To Bedlam and Part Way Back* (1960) and ended with the posthumous *The Awful Rowing Toward God* (1975).

POMEGRANATE BOX 6099 ROHNERT PARK CA 94927

Women Writers

PHOTOGRAPHS BY JILL KREMENTZ

JOYCE CAROL OATES, Princeton, N.J., May 21, 1981
An anomaly in modern literature in that she is prolific, serious, and
unconfined to any genre, Joyce Carol Oates (b. 1938) has averaged two
books of fiction, poetry, essays, or plays per year since 1967. Her novel
Them (1969) won the National Book Award.

POMEGRANATE BOX 6099 ROHNERT PARK CA 94927

Women Writers

PHOTOGRAPHS BY JILL KREMENTZ

MARY McCARTHY, Paris, France, March 21, 1973
Mary McCarthy (1912–1989) showed a "reckless passion for the truth" in
all that she wrote. Her works included biting theater criticism, collected in
Sights and Spectacles (1956); unsparing reminiscences such as *Memories of
a Catholic Girlhood* (1957); controversial novels such as *The Group* (1963);
and probing war reportage from Vietnam.

POMEGRANATE BOX 6099 ROHNERT PARK CA 94927

Women Writers

PHOTOGRAPHS BY JILL KREMENTZ

IRIS MURDOCH, Oxford, England, December 15, 1971
Iris Murdoch (b. 1919) grew up Anglo-Irish in London and attended
school at Oxford. The best known of her twenty-five "novels of ideas"
are *The Severed Head* (1961) and *The Sea, The Sea* (1978), the latter of
which earned Murdoch the Booker Prize.

POMEGRANATE   BOX 6099   ROHNERT PARK   CA   94927

Women Writers

PHOTOGRAPHS BY JILL KREMENTZ

GRACE PALEY, New York, N.Y., February 26, 1974
The daughter of Russian-Jewish immigrants, Grace Paley (b. 1922) was
raised in the Bronx. She has used her experiences, and a modern urban
landscape, to write three volumes of simple, honest, and provocative
stories (*The Little Disturbances of Man, Enormous Changes at the Last
Minute*, and *Later the Same Day*). She is also a tireless activist and teacher.

POMEGRANATE BOX 6099 ROHNERT PARK CA 94927

Women Writers

PHOTOGRAPHS BY JILL KREMENTZ

DOROTHY WEST, Martha's Vineyard, Mass., April 18, 1995
Dorothy West (b. 1907) moved from Boston to New York as a young
woman and became an integral part of the Harlem Renaissance in the
1920s. She founded two magazines, *Challenge* and *New Challenge*, as
outlets for African American writers. In 1994, at eighty-seven, she
published her acclaimed novel *The Wedding*.

POMEGRANATE BOX 6099 ROHNERT PARK CA 94927

Women Writers

PHOTOGRAPHS BY JILL KREMENTZ

ALICE HOFFMAN, Cambridge, Mass., 1995
Alice Hoffman (b. 1952) is the Boston-based author of eleven novels that have—for their lyrical prose and taut storytelling—been dubbed "Yankee magic realism." Her most recent novel is *Practical Magic* (1995).

POMEGRANATE   BOX 6099   ROHNERT PARK   CA   94927

Women Writers

PHOTOGRAPHS BY JILL KREMENTZ

ELIZABETH HARDWICK, New York, N.Y., January 22, 1974
Elizabeth Hardwick (b. 1916) has won accolades as a writer and teacher
(mostly at New York's Barnard College). Though best known for her
incisive literary and social criticism, she may have made her greatest
mark as editor of the eighteen-volume *Rediscovered Fiction by
American Women* (1977).

POMEGRANATE   BOX 6099   ROHNERT PARK   CA   94927

Women Writers

PHOTOGRAPHS BY JILL KREMENTZ

BELL HOOKS, New York, N.Y., October 3, 1995
Born Gloria Watkins, bell hooks (b. 1952) took the name of her great-grandmother (written without capitalization) to "honor the unlettered wisdom of her foremothers." Professor hooks, in her numerous books of essays, has provoked and challenged women with insights into race, gender, and class in America.

POMEGRANATE BOX 6099 ROHNERT PARK, CA 94927

Women Writers

PHOTOGRAPHS BY JILL KREMENTZ

HANNAH ARENDT, New York, N.Y., May 1, 1972
Hannah Arendt (1906–1975) was, at twenty-seven, already a brilliant
essayist and political thinker when Hitler rose to power, an act that not
only sent Arendt into exile but also deeply marked her life's work.
She struggled with this dark epoch in such classics as *The Origins of
Totalitarianism* (1951), *Eichmann in Jerusalem* (1963), and *The Jew
as Pariah* (1978).

POMEGRANATE   BOX 6099   ROHNERT PARK CA 94927

Women Writers

PHOTOGRAPHS BY JILL KREMENTZ

NADINE GORDIMER, New York, N.Y., March 26, 1975
Nadine Gordimer (b. 1923) is a writer of conscience whose novels and
stories of South Africa have, for the past three decades, attacked the
moral corruption of apartheid. For her body of work, she was awarded
the 1991 Nobel Prize in literature.

POMEGRANATE BOX 6099 ROHNERT PARK CA 94927

Women Writers

PHOTOGRAPHS BY JILL KREMENTZ

EUDORA WELTY, Jackson, Miss., May 2, 1972
For the past half century, Eudora Welty (b. 1909) has turned the minutiae
of ordinary southern life into fiction of the highest rank. Though her
Collected Stories (1980) have been compared to Chekhov's, her memoir,
One Writer's Beginnings (1984), gained the wide readership this gentle
American master so richly deserves.

POMEGRANATE BOX 6099 ROHNERT PARK CA 94927